SHAPING THE DEBATE

Defining and Discussing
FREEDOM
OF THE PRESS

Christy Mihaly

ROurke
Educational Media
A Division of

Carson Dellosa Education

ROURKE'S
SCHOOL to HOME
CONNECTIONS
BEFORE AND DURING READING ACTIVITIES

Before Reading: *Building Background Knowledge and Vocabulary*

Building background knowledge can help children process new information and build upon what they already know. Before reading a book, it is important to tap into what children already know about the topic. This will help them develop their vocabulary and increase their reading comprehension.

Questions and Activities to Build Background Knowledge:

1. Look at the front cover of the book and read the title. What do you think this book will be about?
2. What do you already know about this topic?
3. Take a book walk and skim the pages. Look at the table of contents, photographs, captions, and bold words. Did these text features give you any information or predictions about what you will read in this book?

Vocabulary: *Vocabulary Is Key to Reading Comprehension*

Use the following directions to prompt a conversation about each word.

- Read the vocabulary words.
- What comes to mind when you see each word?
- What do you think each word means?

Vocabulary Words:
- anonymous
- authoritarian
- censored
- conservative
- fundamental
- legitimate
- liable
- liberals
- perspectives
- pillar
- preclude
- repression

During Reading: *Reading for Meaning and Understanding*

To achieve deep comprehension of a book, children are encouraged to use close reading strategies. During reading, it is important to have children stop and make connections. These connections result in deeper analysis and understanding of a book.

 Close Reading a Text

During reading, have children stop and talk about the following:

- Any confusing parts
- Any unknown words
- Text to text, text to self, text to world connections
- The main idea in each chapter or heading

Encourage children to use context clues to determine the meaning of any unknown words. These strategies will help children learn to analyze the text more thoroughly as they read.

When you are finished reading this book, turn to page 46 for **Text-Dependent Questions** and an **Extension Activity**.

TABLE OF CONTENTS

News Media: Enemies or Heroes?. 5

Press Highlights Through U.S. History. 10

How the Press Works 17

Student Journalism. 23

News Around the World 29

The Debate over Press Freedom 34

Activity 44

Glossary 45

Index 46

Text-Dependent Questions 46

Extension Activity 46

Bibliography 47

About the Author. 48

The United States Constitution, written in 1787, begins with *We the People* and sets forth a new form of government for a new nation.

CHAPTER ONE

NEWS MEDIA: ENEMIES OR HEROES?

The First Amendment to the United States Constitution guarantees freedom of the press. This protection enables news media to report freely on current events and express their opinions. The protection holds even—and especially—when they disagree with government policy. The nation's founders considered a free press a central **pillar** of democracy.

James Madison drafted the amendments to the Constitution that became the Bill of Rights, effective in 1791. These amendments guarantee basic rights and freedoms including free speech and freedom of the press.

The First Amendment

Congress shall make no law respecting an establishment of religion, or prohibiting the free exercise thereof; or abridging the freedom of speech, or of the press; or the right of the people peaceably to assemble, and to petition the Government for a redress of grievances.

Each December, *Time* magazine names a "person of the year," chosen for their significance in world events. In 2018, *Time* selected "The Guardians"—journalists.

Acknowledging all journalists, *Time* specifically recognized several individuals. These were: Jamal Khashoggi, who was murdered by Saudi agents after his repeated criticism of the government of Saudi Arabia; Wa Lone and Kyaw Soe Oo, arrested for reporting about Myanmar's slaughter of Rohingya Muslims; Maria Ressa, CEO of a news website in the Philippines who reported on killings by police and was then charged with alleged tax evasion which she considered government harassment; and the staff of the *Capital Gazette*, a Maryland newspaper that lost five employees in a gunman's attack on its office. *Time*'s choices highlighted the dangers journalists confront around the world.

Jamal Khashoggi was killed in Istanbul, Turkey, in 2018.

Maria Ressa has been repeatedly arrested.

Time Magazine

Time *magazine was first published in 1923. It offered readers a new weekly news magazine format. Time* covers news about national and international issues, business, science, the arts, and more. Each year, its editors choose a "person of the year" who has had a great influence on the news. They sometimes name a group of people or a thing (such as the personal computer, in 1982).

Some people are critical of the press. Responding to news coverage that he considered unfavorable, U.S. President Donald Trump called the press "the enemy of the American People!" *The New York Times* and others have pointed out that the label "enemy of the people" was historically used by totalitarian leaders such as Germany's Adolf Hitler, the Soviet Union's Joseph Stalin, and China's Mao Zedong, who used extreme **repression** to control their populations.

In an October 2018 tweet, President Donald Trump said, "The Fake News Media, the true Enemy of the People, must stop the open & obvious hostility & report the news accurately & fairly."

Maria Ressa, the journalist in the Philippines, reflected on contrasting views of the press. "I think the biggest problem that we face right now is that the beacon of democracy, the one that stood up for both human rights and press freedom—the United States—now is very confused," she said in an interview with *Time* magazine. She asked, "What are the values of the United States?"

From Printing Press to Internet

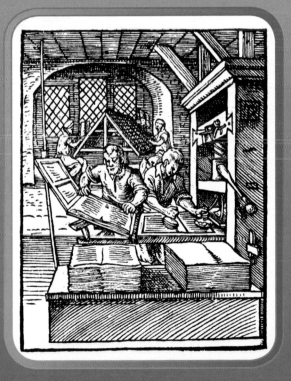

"Freedom of the press" originally referred to the printing press. This 15th century invention vastly increased the public's access to printed news and opinion. The First Amendment barred government interference with the flow of this information. The Constitution's protections now extend to other news media—television, radio, and websites.

German Johannes Gutenberg invented a press that used movable metal letters to print pages instead of carving them into wooden blocks. The Gutenberg press made books and other printed material much less expensive and more available to ordinary people.

CHAPTER TWO

PRESS HIGHLIGHTS THROUGH U.S. HISTORY

In 1798, journalists were jailed for publishing stories criticizing President John Adams. The public outcry against the government's attack on the press helped lead to Adams's defeat in the 1800 presidential election. The new president, Thomas Jefferson, pardoned the journalists.

In 1798, President John Adams signed the Sedition Act, making it a crime to "write, print, utter, or publish" statements opposing the government.

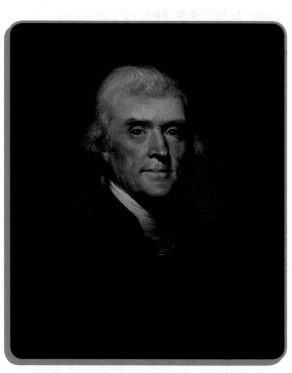

Thomas Jefferson argued that the Sedition Act violated the First Amendment. Jefferson succeeded Adams as president.

As newspapers increased in circulation, their influence grew. In 1898, papers whipped up public support for the Spanish-American War. In the 1900s, investigative journalists called *muckrakers* exposed government corruption and abuses by corporations and pushed for reforms.

In 1898, *Judge* magazine urged readers to remember the U.S. battleship the *Maine*, which exploded in Havana Harbor, Cuba. Because Cuba was seeking independence from Spain, many held Spain responsible and called for the U.S. to go to war against Spain.

By the 1950s, people gathered around the TV rather than the radio for news, sports, and entertainment.

In the 1960s and 1970s, TV coverage helped turn public opinion against the Vietnam War.

In the 1920s, radios began broadcasting entertainment and news. Television followed in the 1950s. By the 1960s, Americans relied more on TV networks' half-hour evening broadcasts than on newspapers for their news. During the Vietnam War, television news brought the war into American living rooms, showing images of destroyed Vietnamese villages and wounded U.S. soldiers. The broadcasts contrasted with official government reports that the war was going well. They horrified people and helped build opposition to the war.

President Richard Nixon (pictured here) tried to discredit Daniel Ellsberg, the former government worker who gave the Pentagon Papers to the *Times*. Nixon's White House sent burglars to steal files about Ellsberg.

Newspapers made headlines in the 1970s. The *New York Times* published the Pentagon Papers, revealing secret government information about the problems in Vietnam. The administration of President Richard Nixon asked a court to halt the publication, to protect national security. The Supreme Court ruled that freedom of the press meant the *Times* and other outlets could publish the documents.

Rather than face impeachment over his illegal activities, Richard Nixon resigned. Vice President Gerald Ford, shown on the left as the Nixon family departs the White House, became president.

The Watergate Scandal

In 1972, two Washington Post reporters investigating a break-in at Democratic Party offices discovered a vast cover-up. President Richard Nixon and his backers were involved in the burglary, and in secret payoffs, political spying, and other "dirty tricks." The White House denied everything. But the reporting was true. Nixon resigned in 1974.

In the 1980s, cable television stations offered 24-hour news and live coverage of events and hearings. Stations developed teams of on-air personalities with varying political opinions to provide commentary. Viewers started choosing news outlets based on their politics. Fox News, with its many **conservative** onscreen newscasters, attracted conservatives. **Liberals** preferred stations with more liberal commentators, such as MSNBC.

With the growth of social media, more Americans started getting news from Facebook and Twitter. Unlike established news organizations, these platforms allowed just about anyone to post almost anything. It became difficult to identify which reports were accurate and which were false.

CHAPTER THREE

HOW THE PRESS WORKS

Code of Ethics

The Society of Professional Journalists (SPJ) promotes ethical journalism, striving "to ensure the free exchange of information that is accurate, fair, and thorough." SPJ has developed a Code of Ethics which provides in part: "Journalists should be honest and courageous in gathering, reporting, and interpreting information."

9:45 AM

What's happening?

⚙ 👤+ Follow

Twitter ✓
@Twitter
Your official source for what's happening. Need a hand? Visit
...ort.twitter.com   ...isco, CA   🎂 Born on March 21
🔗 blog.twitter.com
8M FOLLOWERS

MEDIA   LIKES

To gather information, reporters attend public meetings, seek out expert opinions, interview witnesses, and analyze data. Sometimes they rely on press releases or press conferences. They may follow **anonymous** tips. Journalists often develop professional relationships with sources. They may seek access to public documents. They ask public officials questions—sometimes tough questions. They seek to discover and report the truth.

Jim Acosta, a long-time reporter and CNN's Chief White House Correspondent, often asked tough questions that the Trump White House considered disrespectful.

CNN v. Donald J. Trump: The Jim Acosta Case

At a November 2018 press conference, CNN reporter Jim Acosta asked President Trump questions he didn't like. Trump demanded that Acosta sit down. The White House revoked Acosta's press pass, barring his access to officials and information. CNN challenged this action in court, and the judge ordered the pass returned.

Sometimes, reporters rely on anonymous sources. This is a controversial practice, but journalists contend it's often the only way to get information. A person reporting a crime, for example, may request confidentiality because they fear for their own safety. Journalists may protect a source's identity. However, if a source

violates the law in providing information, the reporter may be legally required to name the source. Reporters have gone to jail in the U.S. for refusing to reveal their sources.

At times, the nation's security depends on keeping information secret. During World War II, newspapers voluntarily **censored** themselves by reporting on the war without releasing information that would harm U.S. military members. U.S. military leaders in the Vietnam War complained that reporters damaged the war effort. In later conflicts in Afghanistan and Iraq, reporters were embedded with troops—traveling with military units in the field. Some journalists hoped embedding would enable them to report accurately. Others worried that the closely controlled access limited their ability to investigate.

Journalists reporting on military activities often face dangerous situations.

Journalists sometimes make errors in reporting. They often issue corrections when errors come to light. When they make mistakes in reporting about public figures, U.S. journalists are generally not held **liable** in court. Public figures cannot recover damages for inaccurate stories unless a reporter knew the information was false or acted with a "reckless disregard" of whether it was false or not. Many find this rule unfair. However, as the Supreme Court has said, it protects the press's ability to inform people about matters of public interest.

In contrast to responsible journalism, fake news is deliberately incorrect and intended to deceive.

CHAPTER FOUR

STUDENT JOURNALISM

The First Amendment doesn't prevent schools from censoring student journalists. In *Hazelwood v. Kuhlmeier*, a high school principal refused to allow articles about divorce and teen pregnancy in a newspaper published by a journalism class. The Supreme Court said that because the newspaper was school-sponsored, the school could control its content. The court warned that school censorship must be based on **legitimate** educational concerns. Schools can't censor items just because they cover controversial topics or criticize school policies.

The U.S. Supreme Court decided the case of *Hazelwood v. Kuhlmeier* in 1988 by a vote of 5 to 3.

The *Hazelwood* rule does not apply to independent student-run media if they function as public forums—places to discuss public opinion. With non-school-sponsored media, schools can usually block only items that are obscene, advocate violence, or seriously disrupt school activities.

Courts give greater protection to communications made in a public forum. Traditionally "public forum" meant a public space such as a street or a park. In the 21st century, cyberspace is an increasingly important public forum.

Private Schools Are Different

*The First Amendment controls only governmental actions affecting freedom of expression, so it doesn't **preclude** restrictions by private schools. Student journalists in private schools must rely on school policies—and some state laws—to protect their press freedom. Sometimes, private school administrators conclude that school censorship is inappropriate or simply "un-American."*

In response to the *Hazelwood* rule, First Amendment activists have proposed state laws to protect student journalists against censorship. More than a dozen states have adopted these "New Voices" laws, protecting freedom of expression for school-sponsored media.

"New Voices" Law Prevents Silencing of Students

In 2018, high school journalists in Vermont reported that the state was investigating one of their school's guidance counselors. The school removed this report from the school website. The students consulted lawyers and fought back. Vermont's "New Voices" law protected their right to publish the story; the school re-posted it.

THE UNIVERSAL DECLARATION
OF Human Rights

WHEREAS recognition of the inherent dignity and of the equal and inalienable rights of all members of the human family is the foundation of freedom, justice and peace in the world,

WHEREAS disregard and contempt for human rights have resulted in barbarous acts which have outraged the conscience of mankind, and the advent of a world in which human beings shall enjoy freedom of speech and belief and freedom from fear and want has been proclaimed as the highest aspiration of the common people,

WHEREAS it is essential, if man is not to be compelled to have recourse, as a last resort, to rebellion against tyranny and oppression, that human rights should be protected by the rule of law,

WHEREAS it is essential to promote the development of friendly relations among nations,

WHEREAS the peoples of the United Nations have in the Charter reaffirmed their faith in fundamental human rights, in the dignity and worth of the human person and in the equal rights of men and women and have

determined to promote social progress and better standards of life in larger freedom,

WHEREAS Member States have pledged themselves to achieve, in co-operation with the United Nations, the promotion of universal respect for and observance of human rights and fundamental freedoms,

WHEREAS a common understanding of these rights and freedoms is of the greatest importance for the full realisation of this pledge,

NOW THEREFORE THE GENERAL ASSEMBLY PROCLAIMS this Universal Declaration of Human Rights as a common standard of achievement for all peoples and all nations, to the end that every individual and every organ of society, keeping this Declaration constantly in mind, shall strive by teaching and education to promote respect for these rights and freedoms and by progressive measures, national and international, to secure their universal and effective recognition and observance, both among the peoples of Member States themselves and among the peoples of territories under their jurisdiction.

ARTICLE 1 —All human beings are born free and equal in dignity and rights. They are endowed with reason and conscience and should act towards one another in a spirit of brotherhood.

ARTICLE 2 —1. Everyone is entitled to all the rights and freedoms set forth in this Declaration, without distinction of any kind, such as race, colour, sex, language, religion, political or other opinion, national or social origin, property, birth or other status.
2. Furthermore, no distinction shall be made on the basis of the political, jurisdictional or international status of the country or territory to which a person belongs, whether this territory be an independent, Trust or Non-Self-Governing territory, or under any other limitation of sovereignty.

ARTICLE 3 —Everyone has the right to life, liberty and the security of person.

ARTICLE 4 —No one shall be held in slavery or servitude; slavery and the slave trade shall be prohibited in all their forms.

ARTICLE 5 —No one shall be subjected to torture or to cruel, inhuman or degrading treatment or punishment.

ARTICLE 6 —Everyone has the right to recognition everywhere as a person before the law.

ARTICLE 7 —All are equal before the law and are entitled without any discrimination to equal protection of the law. All are entitled to equal protection against any discrimination in violation of this Declaration and against any incitement to such discrimination.

ARTICLE 8 —Everyone has the right to an effective remedy by the competent national tribunals for acts violating the fundamental rights granted him by the constitution or by law.

ARTICLE 9 —No one shall be subjected to arbitrary arrest, detention or exile.

ARTICLE 10 —Everyone is entitled in full equality to a fair and public hearing by an independent and impartial tribunal, in the determination of his rights and obligations and of any criminal charge against him.

ARTICLE 11 —1. Everyone charged with a penal offence has the right to be presumed innocent until proved guilty according to law in a public trial at which he has had all the guarantees necessary for his defence.
2. No one shall be held guilty of any penal offence on account of any act or omission which did not constitute a penal offence, under national or international law, at the time when it was committed. Nor shall a heavier penalty be imposed than the one that was applicable at the time the penal offence was committed.

ARTICLE 12 —No one shall be subjected to arbitrary interference with his privacy, family, home or correspondence, nor to attacks upon his honour and reputation. Everyone has the right to the protection of the law against such interference or attacks.

ARTICLE 13 —1. Everyone has the right to freedom of movement and residence within the borders of each state.
2. Everyone has the right to leave any country, including his own, and to return to his country.

ARTICLE 14 —1. Everyone has the right to seek and to enjoy in other countries asylum from persecution.
2. This right may not be invoked in the case of prosecutions genuinely arising from non-political crimes or from acts contrary to the purposes and principles of the United Nations.

ARTICLE 15 —1. Everyone has the right to a nationality.
2. No one shall be arbitrarily deprived of his nationality nor denied the right to change his nationality.

ARTICLE 16 —1. Men and women of full age, without any limitation due to race, nationality or religion, have the right to marry and to found a family. They are entitled to equal rights as to marriage, during marriage and at its dissolution.
2. Marriage shall be entered into only with the free and full consent of the intending spouses.
3. The family is the natural and fundamental group unit of society and is entitled to protection by society and the State.

ARTICLE 17 —1. Everyone has the right to own property alone as well as in association with others.
2. No one shall be arbitrarily deprived of his property.

ARTICLE 18 —Everyone has the right to freedom of thought, conscience and religion; this right includes freedom to change his religion or belief, and freedom, either alone or in community with others and in public or private, to manifest his religion or belief in teaching, practice, worship and observance.

ARTICLE 19 —Everyone has the right to freedom of opinion and expression; this right includes freedom to hold opinions without interference and to seek, receive and impart information and ideas through any media and regardless of frontiers.

ARTICLE 20 —1. Everyone has the right to freedom of peaceful assembly and association.
2. No one may be compelled to belong to an association.

ARTICLE 21 —1. Everyone has the right to take part in the government of his country, directly or through freely chosen representatives.
2. Everyone has the right of equal access to public service in his country.
3. The will of the people shall be the basis of the authority of government; this will shall be expressed in periodic and genuine elections which shall be by universal and equal suffrage and shall be held by secret vote or by equivalent free voting procedures.

ARTICLE 22 —Everyone, as a member of society, has the right to social security and is entitled to realisation, through national effort and international co-operation and in accordance with the organisation and resources of each State, of the economic, social and cultural rights indispensable for his dignity and the free development of his personality.

ARTICLE 23 —1. Everyone has the right to work, to free choice of employment, to just and favourable conditions of work and to protection against unemployment.
2. Everyone, without any discrimination, has the right to equal pay for equal work.
3. Everyone who works has the right to just and favourable remuner-

ation insuring for himself and his family an existence worthy of human dignity, and supplemented, if necessary, by other means of social protection.
4. Everyone has the right to form and to join trade unions for the protection of his interests.

ARTICLE 24 —Everyone has the right to rest and leisure, including reasonable limitation of working hours and periodic holidays with pay.

ARTICLE 25 —1. Everyone has the right to a standard of living adequate for the health and well-being of himself and of his family, including food, clothing, housing and medical care and necessary social services, and the right to security in the event of unemployment, sickness, disability, widowhood, old age or other lack of livelihood in circumstances beyond his control.
2. Motherhood and childhood are entitled to special care and assistance. All children, whether born in or out of wedlock, shall enjoy the same social protection.

ARTICLE 26 —1. Everyone has the right to education. Education shall be free, at least in the elementary and fundamental stages. Elementary education shall be compulsory. Technical and professional education shall be made generally available and higher education shall be equally accessible to all on the basis of merit.
2. Education shall be directed to the full development of the human personality and to the strengthening of respect for human rights and fundamental freedoms. It shall promote understanding, tolerance and friendship among all nations, racial or religious groups, and shall further the activities of the United Nations for the maintenance of peace.
3. Parents have a prior right to choose the kind of education that shall be given to their children.

ARTICLE 27 —1. Everyone has the right freely to participate in the cultural life of the community, to enjoy the arts and to share in scientific advancement and its benefits.
2. Everyone has the right to the protection of the moral and material interests resulting from any scientific, literary or artistic production of which he is the author.

ARTICLE 28 —Everyone is entitled to a social and international order in which the rights and freedoms set forth in this Declaration can be fully realized.

ARTICLE 29 —1. Everyone has duties to the community in which alone the free and full development of his personality is possible.
2. In the exercise of his rights and freedoms, everyone shall be subject only to such limitations as are determined by law solely for the purpose of securing due recognition and respect for the rights and freedoms of others and of meeting the just requirements of morality, public order and the general welfare in a democratic society.
3. These rights and freedoms may in no case be exercised contrary to the purposes and principles of the United Nations.

ARTICLE 30 —Nothing in this Declaration may be interpreted as implying for any State, group or person any right to engage in any activity or to perform any act aimed at the destruction of any of the rights and freedoms set forth herein.

Adopted by the United Nations General Assembly at its 183rd meeting, held in Paris on 10 December, 1948
Issued by U.N. Department of Public Information

UNITED NATIONS

The UN Universal Declaration of Human Rights, adopted in 1948, sets forth the rights that all people inherently possess, including freedom of thought, freedom of opinion, and freedom of expression.

CHAPTER FIVE

NEWS AROUND THE WORLD

The United Nations (UN) has classified freedom of the press as a **fundamental** human right. The UN Universal Declaration of Human Rights states that everyone has the right to freedom of expression, including the right "to seek, receive, and impart information and ideas through any media." Nonetheless, much of the world's population lacks access to freely reported news.

Around the globe, journalists work in difficult circumstances. Several international nonprofit organizations work to support reporters. Among these are Reporters Without Borders and the Committee to Protect Journalists. They fight to free imprisoned journalists and to protect those who are attacked for their work.

Reporters Without Borders brought attention to the plight of two imprisoned French journalists with a sign reading: "For 500 days, Hervé and Stéphane have been hostages in Afghanistan." The pair was released in 2011 after being held by the Taliban for 18 months.

World Ranking

The organization Reporters Without Borders publishes an international ranking each year, evaluating the level of press freedom in 180 countries. In 2019, the top three countries were Norway, Finland, and Sweden. The United States dropped three places, to number 48, based on factors including "violent anti-press rhetoric from the highest level of the U.S. government" and increased danger to journalists.

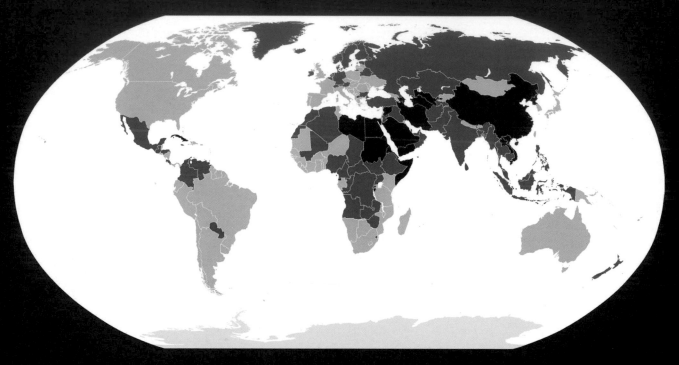

Reporters Without Borders publishes an annual world map, similar to the one shown here, illustrating the situation for journalists by country.

MAP KEY

Very serious situation

Difficult situation

Noticeable problems

Satisfactory

Good situation

Not classified / No data

Under Supreme Leader Kim Jong-un, North Korea ranks as one of the most restrictive countries in the Reporters Without Borders press freedoms ranking. The North Korean government strictly limits communication and harshly punishes violators.

Press repression is widespread in **authoritarian** countries. In North Korea, Kim Jong-un's government controls virtually all information. People receiving unauthorized news can be jailed. Similarly, in Eritrea, only state-controlled media can publish news.

Worldwide in 2018, more than 250 journalists were jailed in retaliation for their work. The Committee to Protect Journalists counted 47 imprisoned in China alone. Governments in other countries, including Saudi Arabia, Ethiopia, Vietnam, and Egypt, restrict what reporters can say in newspapers or on the internet or television. Those publishing unauthorized information are punished.

Pressure from the Committee to Protect Journalists helped convince Paraguay to release journalist Alcibiades González Delvalle, pictured here.

Least Press Freedoms (2019)

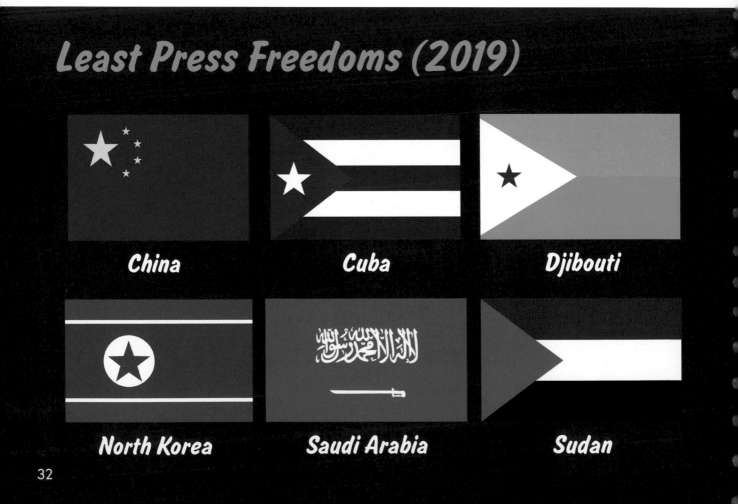

China

Cuba

Djibouti

North Korea

Saudi Arabia

Sudan

Over the Radio

In places with limited access to information, radio broadcasts can provide uncensored news. Radio transmissions from France, for example, carry news into Eritrea, evading censors. Listening can be dangerous, though. In many places, people risk punishment for tuning in. And hostile governments can jam radio signals, effectively silencing them.

More than 50 journalists were killed in 2018. Some died on assignments. Others were murdered by the targets of their investigations, or in retaliation for their reporting.

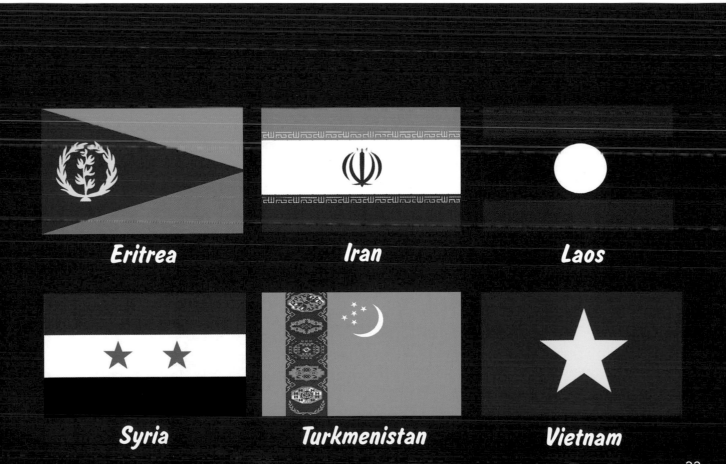

Eritrea

Iran

Laos

Syria

Turkmenistan

Vietnam

CHAPTER SIX

THE DEBATE OVER PRESS FREEDOM

"Fake news" is a major challenge now facing the U.S. press. The term *fake news* means misinformation intended to mislead people. During the 2016 presidential campaign, stories that Hillary Clinton was deathly ill or that Pope Francis had endorsed Donald Trump circulated widely on social media and elsewhere. These were hoaxes.

Kellyanne Conway, Counselor to the President, explained that by "alternative facts," she meant "additional facts and alternative information."

Unfortunately, people believed the false stories. Fake news caused confusion and mistrust. Subsequently, people who disliked legitimate, accurate news reports started calling them "fake news." President Trump's counselor Kellyanne Conway disputed the accuracy of unfavorable reporting and defended the use of "alternative facts." It became harder to identify what was true.

Poor Reporting Can Be Hazardous to Public Health

A 2013 opinion piece in a medical journal argued that flu vaccinations were less effective than many believed. Some media incorrectly reported this as a scientific finding that flu vaccines were ineffective or unsafe. The misinformation caused confusion. Such inaccurate reporting could discourage vaccinations and lead to more flu infections.

Is That True?

Take these steps to avoid falling for a hoax:

- *Follow a range of reliable news sources, not just one.*

- *Consult fact checkers such as PolitiFact, FactCheck.org, and Snopes, which evaluate the accuracy of circulating stories.*

- *Be skeptical. Think critically. Don't spread stories unless you've confirmed they are accurate.*

Another media challenge is consolidation—news organizations combining into a small number of corporations. Analysts worry about consolidation because people hearing news from only a single source don't necessarily get a complete picture. Some journalists believe that with fewer owners, news coverage will not reflect a meaningful diversity of viewpoints. Further, large corporate owners might ignore important local issues. And reporters might avoid stories that could offend corporate owners or advertisers.

HOW TO SP T FAKE NEWS

CONSIDER THE SOURCE

Click away from the story to investigate the site, its mission, and its contact info.

READ BEYOND

Headlines can be outrageous in an effort to get clicks. What's the whole story?

CHECK THE AUTHOR

Do a quick search on the author. Are they credible? Are they real?

SUPPORTING SOURCES?

Click on those links. Determine if the info given actually supports the story.

CHECK THE DATE

Reposting old news stories doesn't mean they're relevant to current events.

IS IT A JOKE?

If it is too outlandish, it might be satire. Research the site and author to be sure.

CHECK YOUR BIASES

Consider if your own beliefs could affect your judgment.

ASK THE EXPERTS

Ask a librarian, or consult a fact-checking site.

IFLA
International Federation of Library Associations and Institutions
With thanks to www.FactCheck.org

One response is to consult alternative media outlets such as local newspapers and community-owned media, nonprofit websites, and advocacy journalism. In advocacy journalism, reporters have an acknowledged agenda, such as environmental protection or family values. Such outlets often lack the money and employees required for comprehensive coverage. But they may provide valuable **perspectives**.

Many websites provide information that supports a specific agenda.

Some critics argue the press has too much freedom. For instance, media outlets may spread unfounded gossip about celebrities. Many believe that this practice serves no legitimate purpose and should be limited. They point out that in other countries, false assertions result in court proceedings and damage awards against the press.

However, U.S. courts place high value on the public's right to know. In 2017, when *BuzzFeed* published documents containing unverified information about Russia's involvement with President Trump, a Russian businessman who was mentioned in the documents sued.

The court rejected his claim for damage to his reputation. Judge Ursula Ungaro explained that when the press gathers and reports on material from government investigations, it acts on the public's behalf. She said the press "provides the public with the information it needs to exercise oversight of the government." In short, while journalists aren't without flaws, the First Amendment protects their freedom to keep the people informed.

We the People *of the United States* ... *Tranquility, provide for the common Defence, promote the general* ... *ordain and establish this Constitution for the United States of* ...

Article. 1.

The 1st Amendment

PRACTICE PREPARING FOR A DEBATE

People explain issues and solve problems through discussion. Debates are formal discussions about an issue. Debate participants present facts they have gathered from reliable sources. They present this information as they try to convince listeners that their opinions about an issue are correct.

Supplies

- paper
- pencil
- books on your topic and/or internet access

Directions:

1. Decide the topic you will research.

2. Write a question that will shape your debate. Example: Should religion be taught in public schools?

3. Write your proposition or opposition statement. Proposition example: Religion should be taught in public schools. Opposition example: Religion should not be taught in public schools.

4. Research your topic using a variety of sources. Make a list of the facts you find and note the source of each fact next to it.

5. Practice presenting your argument.

6. Flip the script! Follow steps 1–5 again, this time preparing with facts that support the other side.

Bonus: Form a debate club with your friends. Assign a new topic regularly. Give each person equal time to present their arguments.

Glossary

anonymous (uh-NAH-nuh-muhs): given by someone whose name is not known or made public

authoritarian (uh-thor-i-TAIR-ee-uhn): requiring strict obedience to the government at the expense of personal freedoms

censored (SEN-surd): removed or withheld information or reports that were considered objectionable

conservative (kuhn-SUR-vuh-tiv): in political views, generally favoring limited government, a strong national defense, and personal freedoms, while opposing large social welfare programs

fundamental (fuhn-duh-MEN-tuhl): basic; very important

legitimate (luh-JIT-uh-mit): genuine; real

liable (LYE-uh-buhl): responsible by law

liberals (LIB-ur-uhlz): generally, people with political views favoring governmental action to address social problems and to seek equal opportunity and equality

perspectives (pur-SPEK-tivz): particular attitudes or ways of looking at things

pillar (PIL-ur): a basic part of a system; something that provides essential support

preclude (pree-KLOOD): to prevent something from happening

repression (ri-PRESH-uhn): the use of force to keep someone or something under very strict control

Index

Committee to Protect
    Journalists 29, 32

fake news 8, 22, 34, 36

First Amendment 5, 9, 10, 23, 25,
    26, 42

Fox News 15

Hazelwood v. Kuhlmeier 23, 24, 26

Nixon, Richard 13, 14

Reporters Without Borders 29, 30, 31

Ressa, Maria 6, 9

social media 16, 34

Time magazine 6, 7, 9

Trump, Donald 8, 19, 34, 36, 42

war 11, 12, 21

Text-Dependent Questions

1. What role did the U.S. news media play during the Vietnam War?
2. What are some ways that reporters obtain information?
3. How can student journalists avoid censorship?
4. What are three countries where press freedoms are limited?
5. What current challenges do the news media face in the United States?

Extension Activity

Imagine you are the editor of your school newspaper. You ask a student reporter to investigate why a former teacher, Mr. Samson, left the school. The reporter finds public records showing that Samson was arrested for theft and is scheduled for trial next month. The newspaper's faculty adviser, Ms. Magenta, is concerned that publishing this information would embarrass Samson. You agree to talk with the school principal before deciding whether to publish the article. What recommendation will you make to the principal, and what arguments will you use to support it?

Bibliography

American Press Institute, "Student Journalism Resources," https://www.americanpressinstitute.org/youth-news-literacy/resources/student-journalism-resources/, (accessed January 9, 2019).

Bill of Rights Institute, "Freedom of the Press," https://billofrightsinstitute.org/educate/educator-resources/landmark-cases/freedom-of-the-press/, (accessed January 9, 2019).

Committee to Protect Journalists, "10 Most Censored Countries," https://cpj.org/2015/04/10-most-censored-countries.php, (accessed January 9, 2019).

DeSmet, Nicole Higgins, "Student Newspaper Censorship: Burlington High School Editors Win First Amendment Battle," *Burlington Free Press*, Sept. 19, 2018.

Gladstone, Rick, "Jailing Hundreds of Journalists Worldwide is the 'New Normal,' Group Find," *The New York Times*, Dec. 13, 2018.

Grynbaum, Michael M, "CNN's Jim Acosta Has Press Pass Restored by White House," *The New York Times*, Nov. 19, 2018.

Light, John, "How Media Consolidation Threatens Democracy: 857 Channels (and nothing on)," Moyers, May 12, 2017. https://billmoyers.com/story/media-consolidation-should-anyone-care/.

Paul, Deanna and Tom Hamburger, "'The Public Has a Right to Know': BuzzFeed Prevails in Russian Tech Mogul's Defamation Suit over Steele Dossier," *The Washington Post*, Dec. 19, 2018.

Reporters Without Borders, "Ranking 2018," https://rsf.org/en/ranking, (accessed January 9, 2019).

Society of Professional Journalists, "Code of Ethics," https://www.spj.org/pdf/ethicscode.pdf.

Vick, Karl, "The Guardians and the War on Truth," *Time*, Dec. 11, 2018. http://time.com/person-of-the-year-2018-the-guardians/.

West, Darrell M, "How to Combat Fake News and Disinformation," Brookings Report, Dec. 18, 2017, https://www.brookings.edu/research/how-to-combat-fake-news-and-disinformation/.

About the Author

Series author Christy Mihaly earned a law degree at the University of California, Berkeley, and worked as an attorney in California and Vermont for more than two decades. Now she exercises her First Amendment rights as a writer. She has published fiction and nonfiction books and articles, poetry, and stories for young readers. Find out more or say hello at her website: www.christymihaly.com.

www.rourkeeducationalmedia.com

PHOTO CREDITS: Cover; drawings of faces© topform | Shutterstock.com, photo© kpboonjit; Page 6 Jamal Khashoggi Editorial credit: HansMusa / Shutterstock.com, page 7 TIME magazines Editorial credit: Elnur / Shutterstock.com; Page 8 Editorial credit: Evan El-Amin / Shutterstock.com; Pages 12-13 people listening to radio Editorial credit: Everett Historical / Shutterstock.com, New York Times Editorial credit: littlenySTOCK / Shutterstock.com; Pages16-17 Facebook login Editorial credit: Pan Xunbin / Shutterstock.com, Twitter page Editorial credit: Denys Prykhodov / Shutterstock.com; Pages 18-19 journalists© FrameStockFootages, male journalists© GaudiLab, Jim Acosta Editorial credit: Evan El-Amin / Shutterstock.com; Pages 20-21 man in suit© PORTRAIT IMAGES ASIA© NONWARIT, hands in cuffs© TonTonic, army© PRESSLAB; Pgae 22© panuwat phimpha, Page 23 Editorial credit: bakdc / Shutterstock.com; Page 24© Monkey Business Images, Page 25 woman© Kirill Shashkov, flag© elic; Page 26 Editorial credit: a katz / Shutterstock.com, Page 27© Andrew Rybalko; Pages 32-33 Flags: Eritrea © Lana2016, N Korea © Globe Turner, Saudi Arabia © Loveshop, Sudan © Juassawa, Djibouti © By S_E, Vietnam © veronchick84, Iran © Loveshop, China © Paul Stringer, Turkmenistan © invisibleStudio, Cuba © Globe Turner, Syria flag © By Destiny Nur; Pages 34-35 FAKE NEWS stamp© wishnuyasa, Hillary Clinton Editorial credit: JStone / Shutterstock.com, Pope Francis Editorial credit: neneo / Shutterstock.com, man with phone© panuwat phimpha; Page 37© JPC-PROD; page 41 tabloid Editorial credit: dennizn / Shutterstock.com; Page 42 Buzzfeed Homepage Editorial credit: 360b / Shutterstock.com, Page 43© zimmytws All images from Shutterstock.com except: Constitution page 4 courtesy of U.S. National Archives and Records Administration; page 5 Madison public domain image (White House Collection); Pages 6 Maria Ressa © Joshua Lim (Sky Harbor); Page 8-9 Hitler © German Federal Archive https://creativecommons.org/licenses/by-sa/3.0/de/deed.en, Stalin and Mao Zedong Public Domain images; Page 10 John Adams Public Domain image source National Gallery of Art, Washington, Jefferson Public Domain image courtesy of the U.S. Government, Pages 12-13 family watching television Public Domain image courtesy of the National Archives and Records Administration, Saigon village in ruins courtesy of U.S. Military, Page 13 Richard Nixon official portrait and page 14 Nixon leaving Whitehouse courtesy of the U.S. government; Page 15 MSNBC logo © BadPiggies https://creativecommons.org/licenses/by-sa/4.0/deed.en; Page 29 leo gonzales https://creativecommons.org/licenses/by/2.0/ Page 30 map © NordNordWest https://creativecommons.org/licenses/by-sa/3.0/de/deed.en; Page 31 Kim Jong-un © Korea.net via https://www.flickr.com/photos/koreanet/41731170961; Page 32 © https://creativecommons.org/licenses/by-sa/4.0/deed.en; Page 36 James McNellis from Washington, DC, United States https://creativecommons.org/licenses/by/2.0/deed.en; Page 39 © IFLA https://creativecommons.org/licenses/by/4.0/deed.en

Edited by: Kim Thompson
Produced by Blue Door Education for Rourke Educational Media. Cover and interior design by: Jennifer Dydyk

Library of Congress PCN Data

Defining and Discussing Freedom of the Press / Christy Mihaly
(Shaping the Debate)
 ISBN 978-1-73161-474-2 (hard cover)
 ISBN 978-1-73161-281-6 (soft cover)
 ISBN 978-1-73161-579-4 (e-Book)
 ISBN 978-1-73161-684-5 (e-Pub)
Library of Congress Control Number: 2019932395

Rourke Educational Media
Printed in the United States of America,
North Mankato, Minnesota